MW01274696

**S**INGLE *parenting*

L I F E ' S   G O L D E N   R U L E S ™

# SINGLE
## *parenting*

### *The Golden Rules for Raising Children Alone*

GENERAL PUBLISHING GROUP
*Los Angeles*

The Life's Golden Rules™ series is published by General Publishing Group, Inc, 3100 Airport Avenue, Santa Monica, CA 90405, 310-915-9000.

Library of Congress Catalog Number 94-079817
ISBN 1-881649-18-0

10 9 8 7 6 5 4 3 2 1

*Sarah Pirch, Editor*
*Cover Design by Nadeen Torio*

PRINTED IN THE USA

# SINGLE *parenting*

1 ◆ Hug your child right now.

2 ◆ An ounce of mother is worth a ton of priest.

3 ◆ One father equals more than a hundred schoolmasters.

4 ◆ You may shoulder the responsibility alone,
   but all the credit will also be yours.

5 ◆ Go to at least two PTA meetings a year.

6 ◆ Get to know your child's teacher. Sometimes kids confide their desires and their fears to a special educator.

7 ◆ Take time to read to and with your young children.

8 ◆ You never divorce your children.

9 ◆ It could be worse. You could be alone
without children.

10 ◆ Bask in the knowledge that your child will
always love you.

11 ◆ It's okay to win at Monopoly, but don't rub it in.

12 ◆ "You can choose your friends, but you only have one mother."     —Max Schulman

13 ◆ Keep a cache of inexpensive new games and toys and take out one or two on rainy days.

14 ◆ Always speak well of the missing parent.

15 ◆ A child must honor both parents. So must you.

16 ◆ Practice forgiving the missing parent.

17 ◆ When you think you can't do it anymore, watch your child sleep.

18 ◆ Parenting, single or otherwise, is not a burden, it is a gift.

19 ◆ A single parent gets twice as much love.

20 ◆ Cook with your children. Then eat with them.

21 ◆ Food is not a substitute for love.

22 ◆ Have a Sunday dinner with as many family members as you can gather together.

23 ◆ Don't make a habit of eating in front of the television—all too soon the kids will be eating pizza with their friends.

24 ◆ "There are times when parenthood seems nothing but feeding the mouth that bites you."

—Peter De Vries

25 ◆ Call your sick child from work.

26 ◆ Whenever possible, take the kids along.

27 ◆ When you're out on the town, call home to talk to the kids before bedtime.

28 ◆ Even a small child can earn a quarter by taking out the trash.

29 ◆ Teach your child to save money for a special toy.

30 ◆ Help your child open a savings account.

31 ◆ Order and routine create security for a child.

32 ◆ Living in the same neighborhood during school years will add to a child's sense of stability.

33 ◆ A regular babysitter makes a child more secure.

34 ◆ Senior citizens make great babysitters.

35 ◆ Let your parents and any other relatives
shower your children with as much love as
they want—it is irreplaceable.

36 ◆ Rent *The Princess Bride*.

37 ◆ Take your kid to a rock concert. Dress casually.

38 • "My best music is understood
by children and animals."

—Igor Stravinsky (1882-1971)

39 ◆ Childish smarting off sounds a lot like adult sarcasm.

40 ◆ Children learn manners from their parents. Mind yours, too.

41 ◆ Teaching your children good manners gives them a tool they can use forever.

42 ◆ Dads can sew buttons on kids' clothes.

43 ◆ Moms can play catch.

44 ◆ Spend some time with your child and grownups of the opposite sex.

45 ◆ Find someone to help you take the kids camping.

46 ◆ "No" means "No"—not giving in to whining.

47 ◆ Kids don't like it when you whine either.

48 ◆ Single doesn't mean alone.

49 ◆ Single parent networking benefits everyone.

50 ◆ Parent's Day at school is a good place to hook up with other single parents.

51 ◆ Find another single parent of the opposite sex for daytime outings.

52 ◆ Teach your child to make scrambled eggs.

53 ◆ Go fly a kite together.

54 ◆ Plant a tiny garden or a window box
together. Watch it grow along with your
child.

55 ◆ Regularly share your accomplishments with each other and write them down.

56 ◆ Make a big deal out of it—even the little things.

57 ◆ When times are tough, you can go over them together.

58 ◆ Go somewhere dressy with your child
as your date.

59 ◆ Go somewhere dressy without the kids.

60 ◆ It's okay to have fun without the kids.

61 ◆ Set aside thirty minutes each day to *listen* to your child.

62 ◆ Your time is the best gift you can give to your child.

63 ◆ Better to be alone and face some problems
than to live with someone who *is* the problem.

64 ◆ One really caring parent can make up for two.

65 ◆ You can get used to having all the pillows on your bed.

66 ◆ Knock before entering your child's room.

67 ◆ When picking a place to live, try to avoid having a common wall between your bedroom and the kids' room.

68 ◆ Holding a frog can turn a Mom into a Princess.

69 ◆ "The greatest love is a mother's, then a dog's, then a sweetheart's."   —Polish Proverb

70 ◆ Insanity is hereditary—you get it from your children.

71 ◆ Children are a test of our spirit.

72 ◆ "I take my children everywhere, but they always find their way home."  —Robert Orben

73 ◆ It's a dull child that knows less than its parent.

74 ◆ There is nothing wrong with teenagers that reasoning with them won't aggravate.

75 ◆ Dr. Seuss calls adults obsolete children. Don't become obsolete.

76 ◆ It behooves you to be blameless if you expect your child to be.

77 ◆ Single parenthood is the greatest preserve of the amateur.

78 ◆ Children ease the loneliness of the single
parent.

79 ◆ Don't make your child the entire focus of
your life. Leave some time for *you.*

80 ◆ Don't blame yourself for being a single
parent.

81 ◆ Buy a small, inexpensive cassette recorder and teach your child to operate it. Make up stories together.

82 ◆ A note in a lunch box will never be traded for junk food.

83 ◆ There is not another parent to run to when you are angry with your child.

84 ◆ You don't have to be both parents at once. Try one at a time.

85 ◆ A single parent must sometimes be mother, father, brother and sister.

86 ◆ Teach your child that nothing is impossible. Then teach yourself.

87 ◆ Remember, it doesn't get any easier. It just gets different.

88 ◆ Share your child's dreams.

89 ◆ Be proud of your kid, and your kid will be proud of you.

90 ◆ Saying "Please" pleases as much as hearing "Please."

91 ◆ Be polite to your child and you'll have raised a polite child.

92 ◆ Know your child's friends. Be one of them.

93 ◆ Learn the names of your child's friends.

94 ◆ Make a special dinner for your child and his or her special friend.

95 ◆ Remember the words of the great single
parent role model Auntie Mame, "Life is a
banquet, and most poor suckers are starving
to death."

96 ◆ In fact, rent *Mame* and watch it alone.

97 ◆ Draw pictures together—you'll be surprised at what you learn.

98 ◆ Always say "Thank You" for the bean art your kid brings home from school.

99 ◆ A child perceived as a burden by the
parent carries a heavy load.

100 ◆ It really is harder on the kids than it is
on you.

101 ◆ "Sorry" is a sponge that absorbs tears.

102 ◆ If you are wrong, admit it. Your child will respect you and you will respect yourself.

103 ◆ If a kid takes sides with the other parent, there may be something wrong with your side.

104 ◆ Whining for the absent parent is natural for a child. It is also natural for you to be hurt by it.

105 ◆ Don't let your child hear you argue with your ex—even over the telephone.

106 ◆ Sometimes the other parent can be a Good Guy, too.

107 ◆ "Before I was married I had three theories
about raising children. Now I have three
children and no theories."

—John Wilmot,
*Rochester,* (1647-1680)

108 ◆ You are not perfect, but you are perfectly you.

109 ◆ When the going gets tough, do something nice for yourself.

110 ◆ Kids can have tough days, too. Let them tell you all about it.

111 ◆ Allow love to flow in both directions.

112 ◆ You can't protect them from everything, but your love is a powerful shield.

113 ◆ There's mother love, and there's smother love.

114 ✦ Respect your own independence and your
child will learn from you.

115 ✦ You are a complete person, in charge of
another complete person.

116 ◆ Don't be afraid to date—practice by going out with friends.

117 ◆ Day camp can be a step in easing the fear of separation.

118 ◆ Older children need reassurance as much as the little ones.

119 ◆ Assure, reassure and repeat.

120 ◆ Buy a set of encyclopedias and learn to use them with your child.

121 ◆ If you don't know the answer, don't fake it. Look it up together.

122 ◆ "Providence protects children
and idiots. I know because I
have tested it."

—Mark Twain (1835-1910)

123 ◆ There is no substitute for shared laughter.

124 ◆ Read *1,001 Stupid Jokes* with your child.

125 ◆ Don't panic if you hear your child use an expression you think is "dirty." Slang changes all the time.

126 ◆ The answer to "Can I ask you a question?" is "Yes."

127 ◆ There should be no question that a child cannot ask.

128 ◆ Some questions don't have pat answers. For example, "Why is there air?"

129 ◆ Try to learn something new every day. Kids learn things every minute.

130 ◆ Don't be afraid to make sensible rules.

131 ◆ If a child is allowed to do anything she wants, eventually she won't want to do anything.

132 ◆ Dinnertime should be the same time on weeknights.

133 ◆ If a child is late for dinner, put it on the table anyway and sit down to enjoy it. You cooked it, they will come.

134 ◆ Anger is not a proper expression when you were actually worried sick about the kid.

135 ◆ Before speaking or striking in anger, count to a million.

136 ◆ Words can be a slap in the face, too.

137 ◆ Ask an angry child to explain the anger.

138 ◆ Time is the most important factor in the
budget of a working single parent.

139 ◆ If there is too little time for your child,
stretch the time you have.

140 ◆ Children are at their best in the morning.
Try to share as much early time as possible.

141 ◆ Get up an hour earlier to share breakfast
with your kids.

142 ◆ Plan bag lunches the night before, but
assemble in the morning.

143 • "Of all the animals, the boy is
the most unmanageable."

—Plato

144 ◆ Kids may not want to play the instrument
you want them to play. This is true in
music and in life.

145 ◆ Kids may play music you hate. Your
parents hated your music too.

146 ◆ Kids should know that it is possible to have lasting relationships.

147 ◆ Your relationship with your child will set the tone for the relationships in his life.

148 ◆ If he wants to get a Mohawk haircut, say "Yes!" He'll get a butch.

149 ◆ If your daughter wants to dress like a grunge, ask her to help pick out the same style for you.

150 ◆ There is no surer way to deflate a teenager's desire for something than for them to find out that you want it too.

151♦ The nastiest word you can call your kid is "Stupid."

152 ♦ The response to a four year old's "I hate you!" is "But I love you!"

153 ♦ Discourage the use of the word "hate," unless if refers to spinach or broccoli.

154 ♦ Never call a child a name you don't want to hear applied to yourself.

155 ◆ "Until a child is one year old,
     it is incapable of sin."

—*The Talmud* (c. 200)

156 ◆ Prepare yourself to answer questions about sex with honesty and sanity.

157 ◆ Sexuality is normal and natural, in children and adults. It is only natural that your kids will ask you about it.

158 ◆ When it comes time to talk about sex,
don't use the birds and the bees. Talk
about human beings.

159 ◆ The truth, in most cases, will do just fine.

160 ◆ Learn to sing your kids' camp songs.

161 ◆ Teach your kids your old camp songs.

162 ◆ Learn the updated version of "Greasy, Grimy Gopher Guts."

163 ◆ Watch the movie *Parenthood*.

164 ◆ Cute puppies grow up to be dogs, but you still have to take care of them. Cute children grow up to be adults, and you don't have to take care of them anymore.

165 ◆ Look after your own parents, and your children will look after you.

166 ◆ The best revenge is to live long enough to be a problem to your children.

167 ◆ If you are widowed, show your children the
photographs of their parents together.

168 ◆ Grieving is natural, but not at the expense
of the child.

169 ◆ Don't let your sense of loss make you withdraw from your child.

170 ◆ The widow or widower should realize how proud the life partner would be to know you are holding the family together.

171 ◆ The time to correct or discipline a child is
immediately after the fact.

172 ◆ Never make excuses to yourself or others
for your child's bad behavior.

173 ◆ It is even more important for the child of a
single parent to dress like the other kids.

174 ◆ Name brand factory outlets can ease the
single parent budget stress of keeping up
with schoolyard fashion.

175 ◆ You can tell a child "We can't afford it," but
first try explaining why they can't have
something in terms of limits.

176 ◆ Never give up.

177 ◆ Never let your kid down.

178 ◆ Never let yourself down.

179 ◆ Mark your child's height with a pencil on
the kitchen wall. Date the marks—time
passes so quickly.

180 ◆ Don't forget to take pictures.

181 ◆ Raise a person, not an appendage.

182 ◆ Single parents and their progeny are bonded by the Krazy Glue of mutual dependence.

183 ◆ Love is the library paste of the art of single parenting.

184 ◆ Make sure they know how to dance.

185 ◆ Read a children's book that was read to you. Then read it to your child.

186 ◆ We are all alone, but we are all alone together.

187 ◆ You will always be the most important
person in your child's life.

188 ◆ Know when to let go, and why.

189 ◆ Rent *Dumbo* and teach your children the gift of flight.

190 ◆ Rent *Pinocchio* and teach your children what it is to be real.

191 ✦ "No" sometimes means "I love you."

192 ✦ You must have discipline in order to impose it.

193 ✦ Someone has to be the grownup.

194 ◆ Try not to express your fear for yourself
or for your children.

195 ◆ Trust is important, but should not be
blind.

196 ◆ Be suspicious of anyone who tries to ingratiate your children before getting close to you.

197 ◆ A date who brings presents for your children is always suspect.

198 ◆ Allow two months before allowing your child to go out alone with someone you are dating.

199 ◆ If in doubt, take your kid with you, and make it a daytime date.

200 ◆ Include your kid in the dating process. Ask opinions about clothes, restaurants and protocol.

201 ◆ If you have had a good time on a first date, share it with your kids. You will want them to do the same for you one day.

202 ◆ The child who initially dislikes your date is usually right.

203 ◆ Recognize when a child becomes jealous of someone you are dating.

204 ◆ Don't date someone who doesn't like children. The kids will know.

205 ◆ Kids have a role in your romantic life.
It's called "Date Monitor."

206 ◆ If your child should catch you kissing your
date goodnight, don't guiltily spring apart.

207 ◆ If your kid thinks your date is a loser,
he or she is probably right.

208 ◆ Don't be tempted to try skateboarding unless you were once a surfer.

209 ◆ Know that there always comes a time when your kid thinks you are hopelessly lame.

210 ◆ Find a subtle way to remind the kids of Mother's Day and Father's Day. It may not matter to you, but it matters to the kids.

211 ◆ A "Happy Father's Day" card is the sweetest tribute of all to a single Mom.

212 ◆ A strong single Dad can be as loving as the Mother of all Mothers.

213 ◆ Let them be what they want to be, not what you wanted to be.

214 ◆ Don't give them everything you never had. Just give them everything you have.

215 ◆ Teach a child about life and he will know how to live it. Teach a child to live, and he will live life.

216 ◆ Don't be alarmed—all little boys want to wear tights and capes at some point. It's a Batman thing.

217 ◆ Don't sweat it. Every child gets potty-trained and stops drinking from a bottle eventually.

218 ◆ Single Dads must remember to respect their daughter's privacy. Especially in the bathroom.

219 ◆ Fathers, if your daughter looks painfully like her mother, remember that half of her is you.

220 ◆ Dads, try not to scare the living daylights out of her first date.

221 ◆ When your child falls in love, it will feel a lot the same to you.

222 ◆ Past is Prologue.

223 ◆ Those who do not remember the past are condemned to repeat it.

224 ◆ The race car driver said, as he ripped off his rear view mirror, "What's behind me is not important!"

225 ◆ "Teach your children well, for the past will surely go by…"  —Crosby, Stills and Nash

226 ◆ The child is father to the man.

227 ◆ If you live in the past, neither you nor your children will have a future.

228 • "My mother had a great deal of
trouble with me, but I think
she enjoyed it."

—Mark Twain

229 ◆ Act like a lady, and your son will be a gentleman.

230 ◆ The daughter of a true gentleman is a lady who will find a gentleman even among brutes.

231 ◆ Never leave your children in the care of someone you would not, in other circumstances, marry.

232 ◆ "You're just like your Mother/Father" can be an insult or a compliment. Only use it as the latter.

233 ◆ Don't stop paying attention to your child's schoolwork just because they're out of grammar school.

234 ◆ A teenaged boy should be shown how to iron a shirt.

235 ◆ Teach your kids to respect the physically challenged.

236 ◆ Children learn bigotry from their parents, even by accident.

237 ◆ Children can learn to imitate you much faster than parrots.

238 ◆ Don't use food as a reward.

239 ◆ Don't make fun of a chubby child.

240 ◆ Don't force them to eat a hated vegetable.
Substitute another that's more palatable.

241 ◆ Take a young child to a carnival before going to a big amusement park.

242 ◆ Teach your child to love animals.

243 ◆ Whenever possible, explain how things work.

244 ◆ Let not the punishment exceed the
misdeed.

245 ◆ Nobody's perfect. Not even your child.

246 ◆ The teen years: 13, 14, 15, Driver's
License, 17, 18, 19.

247 ◆ Teenagers should learn to drive a stick
shift.

248 ◆ When they move out, don't immediately
redecorate their rooms.

249 ◆ Sometimes you will be the parent, sometimes the best friend.

250 ◆ You can't always understand, but always try.

251 ◆ Bolster a teen's confidence. They can never have enough of it.

252 ◆ If the kids always gather at your house it
means you're cool.

253 ◆ Help create a good place to study.

254 ◆ If you can't understand the homework,
don't help. Get a tutor.

255 ◆ Read John Holt's *What Makes Johnny
Fail?*

256 ◆ A child is the ultimate pet.

257 ◆ Your child is not a substitute for your missing mate.

258 ◆ Let them help in the kitchen. Eventually they can cook for you.

259 ◆ Make the holidays festive, even if you have to grit your teeth to do it.

260 ◆ Smile as you remember the words of Martin Mull: "Having children is like having a bowling alley installed in your brain."

261 ◆ Don't repeat a request more than twice. That's called nagging.

262 ◆ When it gets to that point, maximize action and minimize words.

263 ◆ Don't treat all household chores like punishments.

264 ◆ Creativity can ease the pain of a tight budget.

265 ◆ If you can't afford it new, buy it second hand.

266 ◆ In times of no money, lots of little birthday gifts can show how much you care.

267 ◆ Write yourself a congratulatory letter.

268 ◆ Then write your kid one.

269 ◆ The sacrifices will be worth it, especially if you don't complain.

270 ◆ When it's all too much, find a place to watch a sunset.

271 ◆ One conscientious parent can achieve the improbable, if not the impossible.

272 ◆ When you are so tired you can't think, remember how tired you were in the months after the child was born.

273 ◆ You can do anything, but you can't do everything.

274 ◆ To live vicariously through your child is to abandon your own life.

275 ◆ Don't be tempted to live for your children—
let them live for themselves.

276 ◆ Tell your children what you like about them.

277 ◆ Never start a sentence with "You always…"
or "You never…."

278 ◆ In order to teach the value of truth, you must not lie.

279 ◆ Consistency, consistency, consistency— that is the answer.

280 ◆ Don't snoop in their stuff or they will
snoop in yours.

281 ◆ Resist the impulse to read the kid's diary.

282 ◆ Single fathers may be more rare than single mothers, but they face no less a task.

283 ◆ When your friends offer to help out, don't refuse.

284 ◆ When the children are away, it's your chance to play.

285 ◆ A single parent with an only child can still enjoy a good card game of "War" or "Go Fish."

286 ◆ If you have a computer, teach your child to use it. If your child has a computer, learn to use it.

287 ◆ Visit a museum of science and industry together.

288 ◆ Take the kids horseback riding.

289 ◆ Even city kids should see a cow up close at least once.

290 ◆ Keep your sense of humor—you'll need it.

291 ◆ Don't tell your children anything you don't want anyone else to know.

292 ◆ Never betray a child's confidence.

293 ◆ Explain that work is a thing that you do, not just a place that you go.

294 ◆ Always tell a small child that you are leaving and where you are going.

295 ◆ Fear of abandonment will always be there for you and your child. Face your fear and assuage his.

296 ◆ The sons of single moms will be especially
protective. Allow them this expression
of love.

297 ◆ The empty nest is even harder for a single
parent. Feather it with your own
accomplishments.

298 ◆ Remember how hard it was to be a teenager, but resist the urge to tell them about it.

299 ◆ Never say, "When I was your age," unless asked what things were like in "the olden days."

300 ◆ Pets will help you share your love.
And they'll keep your child company
when you're out.

301 ◆ But don't buy a dog unless you are
prepared to take care of it yourself.

302 ◆ Cats are easier.

303 ◆ Responsibility is a relative thing in a teenager.

304 ◆ Sarcasm from the mouths of children can be mistaken for disrespect.

305 ◆ Remember that you are the authority figure.

306 ◆ There will be a time when the kids will say they wish they had a "normal" family. Tell them they have one.

307 ◆ Kids hear stuff about having only one parent. Don't let them use it to get their own way.

308 ◆ "Humor is emotional chaos remembered
   in tranquility."      —James Thurber

309 ◆ "He who laughs, lasts."
                  —Mary Pettibone Poole (c. 1938)

310 ◆ Be the best that you can be. Single parenting is about as close as you can get to Army boot camp.

311 ◆ Always look on the bright side of life.

312 ◆ Learn something new and share it with your child.

313 ◆ A child will rebel no matter what.

314 ◆ Grow with your children.

315 ◆ Teach your children that "Can't Never Did Anything."

316 ◆ "If you think education is
expensive, try ignorance."

—Derek Bok

317 ◆ The relationship between parent and child is not a marriage. It is much more temporary, and much more permanent.

318 ◆ Feel fortunate that you are not separated from your children.

319 ◆ Children are a gift you give to the world. Make sure you wrap it well.

320 ◆ Experience teaches you to recognize a mistake when you've made it again.

321 ◆ The trouble with using experience as a guide is that the final exam often comes first, followed by the lesson.

322 ◆ Moms should go to their kids' sporting events and try to resist running out on the field at the first sign of blood.

323 ◆ Remember—you are the only symbol of their parental pride.

324 ◆ A single Dad's "I love you" can be the best assist a burgeoning athlete will ever receive.

325 ◆ Make sure your kids can swim, even if you can't.

326 ◆ Kids get head lice sometimes. It's not your fault.

327 ◆ If they won't come in out of the rain, invest in rainwear.

328 ◆ Just when you think you can't stand them anymore, kids will do something to make you proud.

329 ◆ Count your blessings. Then multiply them by one hundred.

330 • "Nobody can make you feel inferior without your consent."

—Eleanor Roosevelt

331 ◆ Follow through on promises.

332 ◆ Follow through with plans.

333 ◆ Follow through with punishments.

334 ◆ Kids have bad moods too.

335 ◆ Respect their feelings

336 ◆ Give siblings equal time.

337 ◆ Encourage your children to love and respect siblings—it doesn't come naturally.

338 ◆ Stop smoking. If not for your sake, for your children's.

339 ◆ Say "no" to drugs.

340 ◆ Take care of your own health.

341 ◆ Always pay attention to a child's health complaints.

342 ◆ Running to the doctor every time your child gets a sniffle will create a fearful child, not to mention a wealthy doctor.

343 ◆ Praise a job well done.

344 ◆ Never let 'em see you sweat.

345 ◆ Pat yourself on the back. You deserve it.

346 ◆ Boys need hugs, too.

347 ◆ Allow a boy to become a man and a girl
a woman.

348 ◆ *Fantasia* is a great introduction to classical music—for both of you.

349 ◆ All kids should learn to catch sandcrabs. Be sure to bring sunscreen.

350 ◆ Visit a children's museum together.

351 ◆ Take a train trip together.

352 ◆ Accept a child's apology.

353 ◆ To meet a child on his own level,
you needn't condescend.

354 ◆ Take a trip with your children before they get too old to be seen with you.

355 ◆ When the time comes that your baby doesn't want to kiss you goodbye in front of the school, take it like a champ.

356 ◆ Tell them to save some kicks for later.

357 ◆ Encourage bravery, but discourage
foolhardiness.

358 ◆ Nothing is important enough to keep you from a child's appearance in a school play.

359 ◆ Kids don't always color inside the lines. Neither did Jackson Pollack.

360 ◆ For children, getting caught is the mother of invention.

361 ◆ Never ask a child if he wants to take a bath. Just do it.

362 ◆ Say "no" as a considered response and your child will view it as a sign of your strength as a thoughtful parent.

363 ◆ Protect your children, but not from reality.

364 ◆ Teach your child to treat others the way he would like to be treated. Pass on the first "Golden Rule."

365 ◆ Hug your child again.

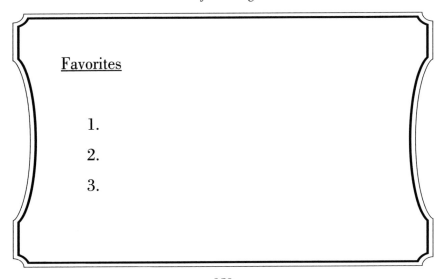

<u>Favorites</u>

1.

2.

3.

4.

5.

6.